50 Irresistibl Dinner Recipes

By: Kelly Johnson

Table of Contents

- Garlic Butter Shrimp Pasta
- Chicken Marsala
- Beef Stroganoff
- Lemon Herb Roasted Chicken
- Creamy Tuscan Salmon
- Spicy Thai Basil Chicken
- One-Pan Lemon Garlic Chicken and Asparagus
- Eggplant Parmesan
- Moroccan Lamb Tagine
- Shrimp Tacos with Avocado Crema
- Vegetable Stir-Fry with Tofu
- Classic Beef Burgers
- Baked Ziti with Spinach and Ricotta
- Stuffed Bell Peppers
- Chicken Fajitas
- BBQ Pulled Pork Sandwiches
- Vegetable Curry with Chickpeas
- Teriyaki Salmon with Broccoli
- Pesto Chicken and Tomato Bake
- Beef and Broccoli Stir-Fry
- Mediterranean Quinoa Bowl
- Chicken Alfredo Bake
- Stuffed Portobello Mushrooms
- Spaghetti Carbonara
- Thai Red Curry with Vegetables
- Honey Garlic Chicken Thighs
- Roasted Vegetable and Hummus Wrap
- Fish Tacos with Mango Salsa
- Baked Lemon Herb Cod
- Classic Lasagna
- Jambalaya with Shrimp and Sausage
- Creamy Mushroom Risotto
- Moroccan Chicken Skewers
- Beef Tacos with Fresh Salsa
- Spinach and Feta Stuffed Chicken Breast
- Ratatouille with Quinoa

- Coconut Curry Shrimp
- Enchiladas with Green Sauce
- Grilled Vegetable and Halloumi Salad
- Sweet and Sour Pork
- Chicken and Broccoli Casserole
- Szechuan Noodles with Chicken
- Chili Con Carne
- Roasted Garlic and Herb Pork Tenderloin
- Vegetable Fried Rice
- Balsamic Glazed Chicken with Vegetables
- Shrimp and Grits
- Spaghetti Aglio e Olio
- Quinoa-Stuffed Acorn Squash
- Braised Beef Short Ribs

Garlic Butter Shrimp Pasta

Ingredients

- 8 oz spaghetti
- 1 lb shrimp, peeled and deveined
- 4 tbsp unsalted butter
- 4 cloves garlic, minced
- 1/2 tsp red pepper flakes
- Salt and pepper to taste
- 1/4 cup fresh parsley, chopped
- Juice of 1 lemon

Instructions

1. **Cook the Pasta:** In a pot of salted boiling water, cook spaghetti according to package instructions. Drain and set aside.
2. **Sauté Shrimp:** In a large skillet, melt butter over medium heat. Add garlic and red pepper flakes; sauté until fragrant. Add shrimp, season with salt and pepper, and cook until pink.
3. **Combine:** Add cooked spaghetti to the skillet, toss to combine, and drizzle with lemon juice.
4. **Serve:** Garnish with parsley and serve immediately.

Chicken Marsala

Ingredients

- 1 lb chicken breasts, sliced
- 1/2 cup all-purpose flour
- 4 tbsp olive oil
- 8 oz mushrooms, sliced
- 1 cup Marsala wine
- 1/2 cup chicken broth
- Salt and pepper to taste
- Fresh parsley, for garnish

Instructions

1. **Dredge Chicken:** Season chicken with salt and pepper, then dredge in flour.
2. **Sauté Chicken:** In a skillet, heat olive oil over medium heat. Add chicken and cook until golden. Remove and set aside.
3. **Cook Mushrooms:** In the same skillet, add mushrooms and sauté until browned. Pour in Marsala wine and chicken broth; bring to a simmer.
4. **Combine:** Return chicken to the skillet and cook until heated through.
5. **Serve:** Garnish with parsley and serve.

Beef Stroganoff

Ingredients

- 1 lb beef sirloin, sliced
- 2 tbsp olive oil
- 1 onion, chopped
- 8 oz mushrooms, sliced
- 2 cups beef broth
- 1 tbsp Worcestershire sauce
- 1 cup sour cream
- Salt and pepper to taste
- Cooked egg noodles, for serving

Instructions

1. **Sauté Beef:** In a skillet, heat olive oil over medium-high heat. Add beef and cook until browned. Remove and set aside.
2. **Cook Vegetables:** In the same skillet, add onion and mushrooms; sauté until tender.
3. **Add Broth:** Stir in beef broth and Worcestershire sauce; bring to a simmer.
4. **Combine:** Return beef to the skillet and stir in sour cream; cook until heated through.
5. **Serve:** Serve over cooked egg noodles.

Lemon Herb Roasted Chicken

Ingredients

- 1 whole chicken (about 4 lbs)
- 4 tbsp olive oil
- Juice of 2 lemons
- 4 cloves garlic, minced
- 2 tsp dried thyme
- 2 tsp dried rosemary
- Salt and pepper to taste

Instructions

1. **Preheat Oven:** Preheat oven to 425°F (220°C).
2. **Prepare Chicken:** In a bowl, mix olive oil, lemon juice, garlic, thyme, rosemary, salt, and pepper. Rub mixture all over the chicken.
3. **Roast Chicken:** Place chicken in a roasting pan and roast for about 1.5 hours, or until the internal temperature reaches 165°F (75°C).
4. **Serve:** Let rest before carving and serve.

Creamy Tuscan Salmon

Ingredients

- 4 salmon fillets
- 2 tbsp olive oil
- 4 cloves garlic, minced
- 1 cup cherry tomatoes, halved
- 1 cup spinach
- 1 cup heavy cream
- 1/2 cup grated Parmesan cheese
- Salt and pepper to taste

Instructions

1. **Sear Salmon:** In a skillet, heat olive oil over medium-high heat. Season salmon with salt and pepper, then sear until golden on both sides. Remove and set aside.
2. **Cook Vegetables:** In the same skillet, add garlic, cherry tomatoes, and spinach; sauté until tomatoes are soft.
3. **Make Sauce:** Pour in heavy cream and stir in Parmesan; cook until thickened.
4. **Combine:** Return salmon to the skillet and coat with the sauce.
5. **Serve:** Serve hot.

Spicy Thai Basil Chicken

Ingredients

- 1 lb ground chicken
- 2 tbsp vegetable oil
- 4 cloves garlic, minced
- 2-3 Thai red chilies, chopped
- 2 tbsp soy sauce
- 1 tbsp fish sauce
- 1 tbsp oyster sauce
- 1 cup fresh basil leaves

Instructions

1. **Cook Chicken:** In a skillet, heat oil over medium heat. Add garlic and chilies; sauté until fragrant.
2. **Add Chicken:** Add ground chicken and cook until browned.
3. **Season:** Stir in soy sauce, fish sauce, and oyster sauce; cook for another 2 minutes.
4. **Add Basil:** Toss in basil leaves and cook until wilted.
5. **Serve:** Serve with rice.

One-Pan Lemon Garlic Chicken and Asparagus

Ingredients

- 4 chicken thighs, bone-in and skin-on
- 1 lb asparagus, trimmed
- 4 cloves garlic, minced
- Juice of 1 lemon
- 2 tbsp olive oil
- Salt and pepper to taste

Instructions

1. **Preheat Oven:** Preheat oven to 400°F (200°C).
2. **Season Chicken:** In a bowl, mix olive oil, garlic, lemon juice, salt, and pepper. Coat chicken with the mixture.
3. **Arrange in Pan:** Place chicken in a baking dish; surround with asparagus.
4. **Bake:** Bake for 25-30 minutes, or until chicken is cooked through.
5. **Serve:** Serve warm.

Eggplant Parmesan

Ingredients

- 2 medium eggplants, sliced
- 2 cups marinara sauce
- 2 cups mozzarella cheese, shredded
- 1 cup Parmesan cheese, grated
- 1 cup breadcrumbs
- 2 eggs, beaten
- Olive oil, for frying
- Salt and pepper to taste

Instructions

1. **Prep Eggplants:** Sprinkle salt on eggplant slices and let sit for 30 minutes to draw out moisture. Rinse and pat dry.
2. **Fry Eggplants:** In a skillet, heat olive oil and fry eggplant slices until golden.
3. **Assemble:** In a baking dish, layer marinara sauce, eggplant, mozzarella, and Parmesan; repeat layers. Top with breadcrumbs.
4. **Bake:** Bake at 375°F (190°C) for 25-30 minutes until bubbly.
5. **Serve:** Let cool slightly before serving.

Moroccan Lamb Tagine

Ingredients

- 2 lbs lamb shoulder, cut into chunks
- 2 tbsp olive oil
- 1 onion, chopped
- 3 cloves garlic, minced
- 1 tsp ground cumin
- 1 tsp ground coriander
- 1 tsp ground cinnamon
- 1 tsp ground ginger
- 1 can (14 oz) diced tomatoes
- 2 cups chicken or beef broth
- 1 cup dried apricots, chopped
- 1 cup chickpeas, drained and rinsed
- Salt and pepper to taste
- Fresh cilantro, for garnish

Instructions

1. **Brown the Lamb:** In a large pot or tagine, heat olive oil over medium heat. Add lamb and brown on all sides. Remove and set aside.
2. **Cook Onions and Spices:** In the same pot, add onion and garlic; sauté until softened. Stir in cumin, coriander, cinnamon, and ginger; cook for another minute.
3. **Add Remaining Ingredients:** Return lamb to the pot, add diced tomatoes, broth, apricots, chickpeas, salt, and pepper. Bring to a boil, then reduce heat to low and cover.
4. **Simmer:** Cook for about 2 hours, or until the lamb is tender.
5. **Serve:** Garnish with cilantro and serve with couscous or bread.

Shrimp Tacos with Avocado Crema

Ingredients

- 1 lb shrimp, peeled and deveined
- 1 tbsp olive oil
- 1 tsp chili powder
- 1/2 tsp garlic powder
- Salt and pepper to taste
- 8 small corn tortillas
- 1 avocado
- 1/2 cup Greek yogurt
- Juice of 1 lime
- Fresh cilantro, for garnish

Instructions

1. **Season Shrimp:** In a bowl, toss shrimp with olive oil, chili powder, garlic powder, salt, and pepper.
2. **Cook Shrimp:** In a skillet over medium heat, cook shrimp for 2-3 minutes per side until cooked through.
3. **Make Avocado Crema:** In a blender, combine avocado, Greek yogurt, lime juice, and salt; blend until smooth.
4. **Assemble Tacos:** Warm tortillas, fill with shrimp, and drizzle with avocado crema.
5. **Serve:** Garnish with fresh cilantro.

Vegetable Stir-Fry with Tofu

Ingredients

- 1 block (14 oz) firm tofu, cubed
- 2 tbsp soy sauce
- 2 tbsp vegetable oil
- 1 bell pepper, sliced
- 1 cup broccoli florets
- 1 carrot, sliced
- 1 cup snap peas
- 2 cloves garlic, minced
- 1 inch ginger, grated
- Cooked rice, for serving

Instructions

1. **Prepare Tofu:** Press tofu to remove excess moisture; then cube and marinate in soy sauce for 15 minutes.
2. **Stir-Fry Tofu:** In a large skillet, heat oil over medium-high heat. Add tofu and cook until golden on all sides. Remove and set aside.
3. **Cook Vegetables:** In the same skillet, add bell pepper, broccoli, carrot, snap peas, garlic, and ginger; stir-fry until tender-crisp.
4. **Combine:** Return tofu to the skillet, stir to combine, and cook for another 2-3 minutes.
5. **Serve:** Serve over cooked rice.

Classic Beef Burgers

Ingredients

- 1 lb ground beef (80% lean)
- 1 tsp garlic powder
- 1 tsp onion powder
- Salt and pepper to taste
- 4 burger buns
- Toppings: lettuce, tomato, onion, pickles, cheese (optional)

Instructions

1. **Form Patties:** In a bowl, mix ground beef with garlic powder, onion powder, salt, and pepper. Form into 4 equal patties.
2. **Cook Burgers:** Preheat a grill or skillet over medium-high heat. Cook patties for 4-5 minutes per side, or until desired doneness.
3. **Toast Buns:** Optional: Toast burger buns on the grill for 1-2 minutes.
4. **Assemble Burgers:** Place patties on buns and top with desired toppings.
5. **Serve:** Serve hot with fries or chips.

Baked Ziti with Spinach and Ricotta

Ingredients

- 12 oz ziti pasta
- 1 jar (24 oz) marinara sauce
- 15 oz ricotta cheese
- 1 cup cooked spinach, drained
- 2 cups shredded mozzarella cheese
- 1/2 cup grated Parmesan cheese
- 1 tsp Italian seasoning
- Salt and pepper to taste

Instructions

1. **Preheat Oven:** Preheat oven to 375°F (190°C).
2. **Cook Pasta:** Cook ziti according to package instructions; drain.
3. **Mix Ingredients:** In a large bowl, combine marinara sauce, ricotta, spinach, Italian seasoning, salt, and pepper. Add cooked ziti and mix well.
4. **Assemble Dish:** Pour half of the mixture into a baking dish, sprinkle with half of the mozzarella, add the remaining ziti mixture, and top with remaining mozzarella and Parmesan.
5. **Bake:** Bake for 25-30 minutes, or until cheese is bubbly and golden.
6. **Serve:** Let cool slightly before serving.

Stuffed Bell Peppers

Ingredients

- 4 bell peppers, halved and seeded
- 1 lb ground beef or turkey
- 1 cup cooked rice
- 1 can (14 oz) diced tomatoes
- 1 tsp Italian seasoning
- Salt and pepper to taste
- 1 cup shredded cheese (optional)

Instructions

1. **Preheat Oven:** Preheat oven to 375°F (190°C).
2. **Prepare Filling:** In a skillet, brown ground meat over medium heat. Drain excess fat. Add cooked rice, diced tomatoes, Italian seasoning, salt, and pepper; mix well.
3. **Stuff Peppers:** Fill halved bell peppers with the meat mixture and place in a baking dish.
4. **Bake:** Cover with foil and bake for 30 minutes. If using cheese, uncover and sprinkle on top, baking for an additional 10 minutes.
5. **Serve:** Let cool slightly before serving.

Chicken Fajitas

Ingredients

- 1 lb chicken breast, sliced
- 2 bell peppers, sliced
- 1 onion, sliced
- 2 tbsp olive oil
- 1 tbsp fajita seasoning
- Salt and pepper to taste
- Tortillas, for serving
- Toppings: sour cream, salsa, guacamole

Instructions

1. **Sauté Chicken:** In a skillet, heat olive oil over medium heat. Add chicken and season with fajita seasoning, salt, and pepper; cook until browned.
2. **Add Vegetables:** Add bell peppers and onion; sauté until softened.
3. **Serve:** Serve hot with tortillas and desired toppings.

BBQ Pulled Pork Sandwiches

Ingredients

- 2 lbs pork shoulder
- 1 cup BBQ sauce
- 1 onion, sliced
- 4 hamburger buns
- Coleslaw, for topping

Instructions

1. **Slow Cook Pork:** Place pork shoulder and onion in a slow cooker; cover with BBQ sauce. Cook on low for 8 hours, or until tender.
2. **Shred Pork:** Remove pork from the slow cooker and shred with two forks. Return to the cooker to mix with sauce.
3. **Assemble Sandwiches:** Serve pulled pork on hamburger buns topped with coleslaw.
4. **Enjoy:** Serve hot.

Vegetable Curry with Chickpeas

Ingredients

- 1 can (15 oz) chickpeas, drained and rinsed
- 1 onion, chopped
- 2 cloves garlic, minced
- 1 inch ginger, grated
- 1 bell pepper, chopped
- 1 zucchini, chopped
- 1 can (14 oz) coconut milk
- 2 tbsp curry powder
- 1 tsp cumin
- Salt and pepper to taste
- Fresh cilantro, for garnish
- Cooked rice, for serving

Instructions

1. **Sauté Aromatics:** In a large pot, heat oil over medium heat. Add onion, garlic, and ginger; sauté until softened.
2. **Add Vegetables and Spices:** Stir in bell pepper and zucchini; cook for a few minutes. Add curry powder, cumin, salt, and pepper.
3. **Add Chickpeas and Coconut Milk:** Stir in chickpeas and coconut milk; bring to a simmer. Cook for 15-20 minutes, stirring occasionally.
4. **Serve:** Garnish with cilantro and serve over cooked rice.

Teriyaki Salmon with Broccoli

Ingredients

- 4 salmon fillets
- 1 cup broccoli florets
- 1/4 cup teriyaki sauce
- 2 tbsp olive oil
- Sesame seeds, for garnish
- Cooked rice, for serving

Instructions

1. **Preheat Oven:** Preheat oven to 400°F (200°C).
2. **Prepare Salmon:** Place salmon on a baking sheet lined with parchment paper. Brush with teriyaki sauce.
3. **Add Broccoli:** Toss broccoli with olive oil, salt, and pepper; arrange around salmon.
4. **Bake:** Bake for 15-20 minutes, until salmon is cooked through and broccoli is tender.
5. **Serve:** Garnish with sesame seeds and serve over cooked rice.

Pesto Chicken and Tomato Bake

Ingredients

- 4 chicken breasts
- 1 cup cherry tomatoes, halved
- 1/2 cup pesto sauce
- 1 cup mozzarella cheese, shredded
- Salt and pepper to taste

Instructions

1. **Preheat Oven:** Preheat oven to 375°F (190°C).
2. **Prepare Chicken:** Place chicken breasts in a baking dish; season with salt and pepper.
3. **Add Pesto and Tomatoes:** Spread pesto over chicken and top with cherry tomatoes.
4. **Bake:** Bake for 25-30 minutes. During the last 5 minutes, sprinkle with mozzarella cheese and return to the oven until melted.
5. **Serve:** Serve hot with a side salad or pasta.

Beef and Broccoli Stir-Fry

Ingredients

- 1 lb beef, thinly sliced
- 2 cups broccoli florets
- 2 tbsp soy sauce
- 1 tbsp oyster sauce
- 2 cloves garlic, minced
- 1 tbsp ginger, grated
- 2 tbsp vegetable oil
- Cooked rice, for serving

Instructions

1. **Marinate Beef:** In a bowl, combine beef with soy sauce and oyster sauce; let marinate for 15 minutes.
2. **Stir-Fry Beef:** In a large skillet or wok, heat oil over medium-high heat. Add beef and cook until browned; remove and set aside.
3. **Cook Broccoli:** In the same skillet, add broccoli, garlic, and ginger; stir-fry until broccoli is tender.
4. **Combine:** Return beef to the skillet and stir to combine; cook for another minute.
5. **Serve:** Serve over cooked rice.

Mediterranean Quinoa Bowl

Ingredients

- 1 cup quinoa, rinsed
- 2 cups vegetable broth
- 1 cucumber, diced
- 1 cup cherry tomatoes, halved
- 1/2 cup Kalamata olives, pitted and halved
- 1/4 cup feta cheese, crumbled
- 2 tbsp olive oil
- Juice of 1 lemon
- Salt and pepper to taste

Instructions

1. **Cook Quinoa:** In a saucepan, combine quinoa and vegetable broth; bring to a boil. Reduce heat, cover, and simmer for 15 minutes, or until liquid is absorbed.
2. **Prepare Vegetables:** In a large bowl, combine cucumber, cherry tomatoes, olives, and feta.
3. **Mix Quinoa and Dressing:** Fluff cooked quinoa with a fork; add to the vegetable mixture. Drizzle with olive oil, lemon juice, salt, and pepper; toss to combine.
4. **Serve:** Serve chilled or at room temperature.

Chicken Alfredo Bake

Ingredients

- 3 cups cooked rotini pasta
- 2 cups cooked chicken, shredded
- 2 cups Alfredo sauce
- 1 cup mozzarella cheese, shredded
- 1/2 cup Parmesan cheese, grated
- Fresh parsley, for garnish

Instructions

1. **Preheat Oven:** Preheat oven to 350°F (175°C).
2. **Combine Ingredients:** In a large bowl, combine cooked pasta, chicken, Alfredo sauce, and half of the mozzarella cheese.
3. **Transfer to Baking Dish:** Pour mixture into a greased baking dish. Top with remaining mozzarella and Parmesan cheese.
4. **Bake:** Bake for 25-30 minutes, until cheese is bubbly and golden.
5. **Serve:** Garnish with parsley before serving.

Stuffed Portobello Mushrooms

Ingredients

- 4 large portobello mushrooms
- 1 cup cooked quinoa
- 1/2 cup cherry tomatoes, diced
- 1/2 cup spinach, chopped
- 1/4 cup feta cheese, crumbled
- 2 tbsp olive oil
- Salt and pepper to taste

Instructions

1. **Preheat Oven:** Preheat oven to 375°F (190°C).
2. **Prepare Mushrooms:** Remove stems from mushrooms and brush caps with olive oil; place on a baking sheet.
3. **Make Filling:** In a bowl, combine cooked quinoa, cherry tomatoes, spinach, feta, salt, and pepper.
4. **Stuff Mushrooms:** Fill each mushroom cap with the quinoa mixture.
5. **Bake:** Bake for 20-25 minutes until mushrooms are tender.
6. **Serve:** Serve warm as an appetizer or main dish.

Spaghetti Carbonara

Ingredients

- 12 oz spaghetti
- 4 oz pancetta or bacon, diced
- 2 large eggs
- 1/2 cup grated Parmesan cheese
- 2 cloves garlic, minced
- Salt and pepper to taste
- Fresh parsley, for garnish

Instructions

1. **Cook Spaghetti:** Cook spaghetti according to package instructions; reserve 1 cup pasta water, then drain.
2. **Cook Pancetta:** In a large skillet, cook pancetta over medium heat until crispy. Add garlic and cook for 1 minute.
3. **Combine Ingredients:** In a bowl, whisk together eggs and Parmesan. Add hot spaghetti to the skillet with pancetta; remove from heat and quickly stir in egg mixture, adding reserved pasta water as needed to create a creamy sauce.
4. **Serve:** Season with salt and pepper; garnish with parsley before serving.

Thai Red Curry with Vegetables

Ingredients

- 1 can (14 oz) coconut milk
- 2 tbsp red curry paste
- 2 cups mixed vegetables (bell peppers, broccoli, carrots)
- 1 cup snap peas
- 1 tbsp soy sauce
- 1 tbsp lime juice
- Fresh basil or cilantro, for garnish
- Cooked rice, for serving

Instructions

1. **Heat Coconut Milk:** In a large pot, heat coconut milk over medium heat.
2. **Add Curry Paste:** Stir in red curry paste and cook for 2-3 minutes until fragrant.
3. **Add Vegetables:** Add mixed vegetables and snap peas; cook until tender, about 5-7 minutes.
4. **Season:** Stir in soy sauce and lime juice.
5. **Serve:** Garnish with fresh basil or cilantro and serve over cooked rice.

Honey Garlic Chicken Thighs

Ingredients

- 4 chicken thighs, bone-in and skin-on
- 1/4 cup honey
- 3 cloves garlic, minced
- 2 tbsp soy sauce
- 1 tbsp olive oil
- Salt and pepper to taste
- Fresh parsley, for garnish

Instructions

1. **Preheat Oven:** Preheat oven to 400°F (200°C).
2. **Prepare Sauce:** In a bowl, mix honey, garlic, soy sauce, olive oil, salt, and pepper.
3. **Coat Chicken:** Place chicken thighs in a baking dish; pour honey garlic sauce over the top.
4. **Bake:** Bake for 35-40 minutes, basting with sauce halfway through, until chicken is cooked through.
5. **Serve:** Garnish with parsley before serving.

Roasted Vegetable and Hummus Wrap

Ingredients

- 1 cup mixed vegetables (zucchini, bell peppers, carrots), chopped
- 2 tbsp olive oil
- Salt and pepper to taste
- 4 whole wheat wraps
- 1 cup hummus
- Fresh spinach or arugula

Instructions

1. **Preheat Oven:** Preheat oven to 425°F (220°C).
2. **Roast Vegetables:** Toss chopped vegetables with olive oil, salt, and pepper; spread on a baking sheet and roast for 20-25 minutes.
3. **Assemble Wrap:** Spread hummus over each wrap, top with roasted vegetables and fresh spinach.
4. **Roll and Serve:** Roll up the wraps and slice in half to serve.

Fish Tacos with Mango Salsa

Ingredients

- 1 lb white fish (tilapia or cod)
- 1 tbsp olive oil
- 1 tsp chili powder
- 1/2 tsp cumin
- Salt and pepper to taste
- 8 small corn tortillas

For Mango Salsa:

- 1 ripe mango, diced
- 1/4 red onion, chopped
- 1 jalapeño, seeded and chopped
- Juice of 1 lime
- Salt to taste

Instructions

1. **Prepare Salsa:** In a bowl, combine mango, red onion, jalapeño, lime juice, and salt; set aside.
2. **Cook Fish:** Season fish with olive oil, chili powder, cumin, salt, and pepper. Cook in a skillet over medium heat for 3-4 minutes per side until cooked through.
3. **Warm Tortillas:** Warm corn tortillas in a dry skillet or microwave.
4. **Assemble Tacos:** Flake fish and place in tortillas; top with mango salsa.
5. **Serve:** Serve immediately with lime wedges.

Baked Lemon Herb Cod

Ingredients

- 4 cod fillets
- 2 tbsp olive oil
- Juice of 1 lemon
- 1 tsp dried thyme
- 1 tsp garlic powder
- Salt and pepper to taste

Instructions

1. **Preheat Oven:** Preheat oven to 375°F (190°C).
2. **Prepare Baking Dish:** Place cod fillets in a greased baking dish.
3. **Make Marinade:** In a small bowl, whisk together olive oil, lemon juice, thyme, garlic powder, salt, and pepper.
4. **Coat Cod:** Pour marinade over the cod fillets.
5. **Bake:** Bake for 15-20 minutes until cod is opaque and flakes easily with a fork.

Classic Lasagna

Ingredients

- 12 lasagna noodles
- 2 cups ricotta cheese
- 2 cups mozzarella cheese, shredded
- 1 cup Parmesan cheese, grated
- 1 jar (24 oz) marinara sauce
- 1 lb ground beef or sausage, cooked
- 1 egg
- Salt and pepper to taste
- Fresh basil, for garnish

Instructions

1. **Cook Noodles:** Cook lasagna noodles according to package instructions; drain and set aside.
2. **Mix Cheese Filling:** In a bowl, combine ricotta cheese, egg, salt, and pepper.
3. **Assemble Lasagna:** In a baking dish, spread a layer of marinara sauce, then layer noodles, ricotta mixture, cooked meat, and mozzarella. Repeat layers, ending with marinara sauce and mozzarella on top.
4. **Bake:** Cover with foil and bake at 375°F (190°C) for 25 minutes. Remove foil and bake for another 15 minutes until cheese is bubbly.
5. **Serve:** Let it cool for a few minutes before slicing; garnish with fresh basil.

Jambalaya with Shrimp and Sausage

Ingredients

- 1 lb shrimp, peeled and deveined
- 1 lb smoked sausage, sliced
- 1 onion, chopped
- 1 bell pepper, chopped
- 2 celery stalks, chopped
- 4 cloves garlic, minced
- 1 can (14 oz) diced tomatoes
- 2 cups chicken broth
- 1 cup long-grain rice
- 2 tbsp Cajun seasoning
- Salt and pepper to taste
- Green onions, for garnish

Instructions

1. **Sauté Vegetables:** In a large pot, sauté onion, bell pepper, celery, and garlic until softened.
2. **Add Sausage:** Stir in sliced sausage and cook until browned.
3. **Combine Ingredients:** Add diced tomatoes, chicken broth, rice, Cajun seasoning, salt, and pepper. Bring to a boil.
4. **Simmer:** Reduce heat, cover, and simmer for 20-25 minutes until rice is cooked.
5. **Add Shrimp:** Stir in shrimp and cook for another 5 minutes until shrimp are pink and cooked through.
6. **Serve:** Garnish with green onions before serving.

Creamy Mushroom Risotto

Ingredients

- 1 cup Arborio rice
- 4 cups chicken or vegetable broth
- 1 cup mushrooms, sliced
- 1 onion, chopped
- 2 cloves garlic, minced
- 1/2 cup Parmesan cheese, grated
- 2 tbsp olive oil
- Salt and pepper to taste
- Fresh parsley, for garnish

Instructions

1. **Heat Broth:** In a saucepan, heat broth and keep warm on low heat.
2. **Sauté Vegetables:** In a large pan, heat olive oil over medium heat. Add onion and garlic; sauté until softened. Add mushrooms and cook until browned.
3. **Add Rice:** Stir in Arborio rice and cook for 1-2 minutes until lightly toasted.
4. **Add Broth Gradually:** Begin adding warm broth, one ladle at a time, stirring constantly until absorbed before adding more. Continue until rice is creamy and al dente (about 18-20 minutes).
5. **Finish Risotto:** Stir in Parmesan cheese, salt, and pepper.
6. **Serve:** Garnish with fresh parsley before serving.

Moroccan Chicken Skewers

Ingredients

- 1 lb chicken breast, cut into cubes
- 2 tbsp olive oil
- 1 tbsp ground cumin
- 1 tbsp paprika
- 1 tsp cinnamon
- Salt and pepper to taste
- 1 lemon, juiced
- Fresh parsley, for garnish

Instructions

1. **Marinate Chicken:** In a bowl, mix olive oil, cumin, paprika, cinnamon, salt, pepper, and lemon juice. Add chicken cubes and marinate for at least 30 minutes.
2. **Preheat Grill:** Preheat the grill to medium-high heat.
3. **Skewer Chicken:** Thread marinated chicken onto skewers.
4. **Grill:** Grill skewers for about 10-12 minutes, turning occasionally until cooked through.
5. **Serve:** Garnish with fresh parsley before serving.

Beef Tacos with Fresh Salsa

Ingredients

- 1 lb ground beef
- 1 tsp taco seasoning
- 8 small corn tortillas
- 1 cup fresh salsa (tomatoes, onion, cilantro, lime juice)
- Shredded lettuce and cheese for toppings

Instructions

1. **Cook Beef:** In a skillet, cook ground beef over medium heat until browned. Add taco seasoning and stir well.
2. **Warm Tortillas:** Warm corn tortillas in a dry skillet or microwave.
3. **Assemble Tacos:** Fill each tortilla with beef and top with fresh salsa, lettuce, and cheese.
4. **Serve:** Serve immediately with lime wedges.

Spinach and Feta Stuffed Chicken Breast

Ingredients

- 4 chicken breasts
- 1 cup spinach, wilted
- 1/2 cup feta cheese, crumbled
- 2 cloves garlic, minced
- Salt and pepper to taste
- Olive oil for drizzling

Instructions

1. **Preheat Oven:** Preheat oven to 375°F (190°C).
2. **Prepare Filling:** In a bowl, combine wilted spinach, feta cheese, garlic, salt, and pepper.
3. **Stuff Chicken:** Cut a pocket in each chicken breast and stuff with the spinach mixture.
4. **Bake:** Place stuffed chicken in a baking dish, drizzle with olive oil, and bake for 25-30 minutes until cooked through.
5. **Serve:** Let rest for a few minutes before slicing to serve.

Ratatouille with Quinoa

Ingredients

- 1 zucchini, chopped
- 1 eggplant, chopped
- 1 bell pepper, chopped
- 1 onion, chopped
- 2 cloves garlic, minced
- 1 can (14 oz) diced tomatoes
- 1 cup quinoa, cooked
- Olive oil, salt, and pepper to taste

Instructions

1. **Sauté Vegetables:** In a large skillet, heat olive oil and sauté onion and garlic until translucent.
2. **Add Veggies:** Add zucchini, eggplant, and bell pepper; cook until softened.
3. **Add Tomatoes:** Stir in diced tomatoes, salt, and pepper. Simmer for about 10 minutes.
4. **Combine with Quinoa:** Serve ratatouille over cooked quinoa.

Coconut Curry Shrimp

Ingredients

- 1 lb shrimp, peeled and deveined
- 1 can (14 oz) coconut milk
- 2 tbsp red curry paste
- 1 bell pepper, sliced
- 2 cups spinach
- 2 tbsp lime juice
- Salt to taste

Instructions

1. **Heat Coconut Milk:** In a pan, heat coconut milk and stir in red curry paste.
2. **Add Shrimp and Veggies:** Add shrimp and bell pepper; cook for 5-7 minutes until shrimp are pink.
3. **Add Spinach:** Stir in spinach and cook until wilted.
4. **Finish:** Add lime juice and salt to taste before serving.

Enchiladas with Green Sauce

Ingredients

- 8 corn tortillas
- 2 cups cooked shredded chicken
- 1 can (14 oz) green enchilada sauce
- 1 cup shredded cheese
- 1/2 cup sour cream for serving
- Chopped cilantro for garnish

Instructions

1. **Preheat Oven:** Preheat oven to 350°F (175°C).
2. **Fill Tortillas:** Fill each tortilla with shredded chicken and roll up.
3. **Arrange in Dish:** Place enchiladas seam side down in a baking dish.
4. **Top with Sauce and Cheese:** Pour green enchilada sauce over the top and sprinkle with cheese.
5. **Bake:** Bake for 20-25 minutes until heated through and cheese is melted.
6. **Serve:** Garnish with sour cream and cilantro.

Grilled Vegetable and Halloumi Salad

Ingredients

- 1 block (8 oz) halloumi cheese, sliced
- 1 zucchini, sliced
- 1 bell pepper, sliced
- 1 red onion, sliced
- 2 tbsp olive oil
- Mixed greens for serving
- Balsamic vinaigrette for dressing

Instructions

1. **Preheat Grill:** Preheat grill to medium-high heat.
2. **Grill Vegetables:** Toss vegetables with olive oil, salt, and pepper; grill until tender and slightly charred.
3. **Grill Halloumi:** Grill halloumi slices for 2-3 minutes per side until golden.
4. **Assemble Salad:** Serve grilled vegetables and halloumi over mixed greens and drizzle with balsamic vinaigrette.

Sweet and Sour Pork

Ingredients

- 1 lb pork tenderloin, cubed
- 1 bell pepper, chopped
- 1 onion, chopped
- 1 cup pineapple chunks
- 1/2 cup sweet and sour sauce
- 2 tbsp cornstarch
- Olive oil for frying

Instructions

1. **Coat Pork:** Toss cubed pork in cornstarch until coated.
2. **Heat Oil:** In a skillet, heat olive oil over medium heat; add pork and cook until browned.
3. **Add Vegetables:** Stir in bell pepper, onion, and pineapple; cook until vegetables are tender.
4. **Add Sauce:** Pour sweet and sour sauce over the mixture and cook for an additional 5 minutes.
5. **Serve:** Serve hot over rice.

Chicken and Broccoli Casserole

Ingredients

- 2 cups cooked chicken, shredded
- 2 cups broccoli florets, steamed
- 1 cup cooked rice
- 1 can (10.5 oz) cream of mushroom soup
- 1 cup shredded cheddar cheese
- 1/2 cup milk
- 1 tsp garlic powder
- Salt and pepper to taste

Instructions

1. **Preheat Oven:** Preheat oven to 350°F (175°C).
2. **Mix Ingredients:** In a large bowl, combine shredded chicken, steamed broccoli, cooked rice, cream of mushroom soup, milk, garlic powder, salt, and pepper.
3. **Transfer to Baking Dish:** Pour the mixture into a greased casserole dish and top with shredded cheddar cheese.
4. **Bake:** Bake for 25-30 minutes until heated through and cheese is bubbly.

Szechuan Noodles with Chicken

Ingredients

- 8 oz noodles (such as spaghetti or udon)
- 1 lb chicken breast, sliced
- 2 tbsp Szechuan sauce
- 2 cups mixed vegetables (bell pepper, carrots, snow peas)
- 2 cloves garlic, minced
- 2 tbsp soy sauce
- 2 tbsp sesame oil

Instructions

1. **Cook Noodles:** Cook noodles according to package instructions; drain and set aside.
2. **Stir-Fry Chicken:** In a large skillet, heat sesame oil over medium-high heat; add garlic and sliced chicken. Cook until chicken is browned.
3. **Add Vegetables:** Stir in mixed vegetables and cook for an additional 3-4 minutes until tender.
4. **Combine:** Add cooked noodles and Szechuan sauce, tossing to combine. Serve hot.

Chili Con Carne

Ingredients

- 1 lb ground beef
- 1 can (15 oz) kidney beans, drained
- 1 can (15 oz) diced tomatoes
- 1 onion, chopped
- 2 cloves garlic, minced
- 2 tbsp chili powder
- 1 tsp cumin
- Salt and pepper to taste

Instructions

1. **Cook Beef:** In a large pot, brown ground beef over medium heat; drain excess fat.
2. **Add Onions and Garlic:** Stir in chopped onion and garlic, cooking until softened.
3. **Add Remaining Ingredients:** Add kidney beans, diced tomatoes, chili powder, cumin, salt, and pepper.
4. **Simmer:** Bring to a simmer and cook for 20-30 minutes, stirring occasionally. Serve hot.

Roasted Garlic and Herb Pork Tenderloin

Ingredients

- 1 lb pork tenderloin
- 4 cloves garlic, minced
- 2 tbsp olive oil
- 1 tsp dried thyme
- 1 tsp rosemary
- Salt and pepper to taste

Instructions

1. **Preheat Oven:** Preheat oven to 400°F (200°C).
2. **Prepare Marinade:** In a small bowl, mix garlic, olive oil, thyme, rosemary, salt, and pepper.
3. **Marinate Pork:** Rub the marinade over the pork tenderloin.
4. **Roast:** Place in a baking dish and roast for 25-30 minutes, or until the internal temperature reaches 145°F (63°C). Let rest before slicing.

Vegetable Fried Rice

Ingredients

- 3 cups cooked rice
- 1 cup mixed vegetables (peas, carrots, corn)
- 2 eggs, beaten
- 2 tbsp soy sauce
- 2 green onions, sliced
- 2 tbsp sesame oil

Instructions

1. **Heat Oil:** In a large skillet, heat sesame oil over medium heat.
2. **Add Vegetables:** Stir in mixed vegetables and cook until heated through.
3. **Add Rice:** Add cooked rice and soy sauce, mixing well.
4. **Scramble Eggs:** Push rice to one side and add beaten eggs, scrambling until cooked. Stir in green onions before serving.

Balsamic Glazed Chicken with Vegetables

Ingredients

- 4 chicken breasts
- 2 cups mixed vegetables (zucchini, bell peppers, carrots)
- 1/2 cup balsamic vinegar
- 2 tbsp honey
- Salt and pepper to taste
- Olive oil for drizzling

Instructions

1. **Preheat Oven:** Preheat oven to 375°F (190°C).
2. **Prepare Glaze:** In a small bowl, mix balsamic vinegar, honey, salt, and pepper.
3. **Arrange Chicken:** Place chicken breasts in a baking dish and surround with mixed vegetables. Drizzle with olive oil and balsamic glaze.
4. **Bake:** Bake for 25-30 minutes until chicken is cooked through.

Shrimp and Grits

Ingredients

- 1 lb shrimp, peeled and deveined
- 1 cup grits
- 4 cups water or chicken broth
- 4 slices bacon, chopped
- 2 cloves garlic, minced
- 1/2 cup shredded cheddar cheese
- Salt and pepper to taste

Instructions

1. **Cook Grits:** In a pot, bring water or broth to a boil; stir in grits and cook until thickened. Stir in cheese, salt, and pepper.
2. **Cook Bacon:** In a skillet, cook bacon until crispy; remove and set aside.
3. **Sauté Shrimp:** In the same skillet, add shrimp and garlic, cooking until shrimp are pink.
4. **Serve:** Serve shrimp over grits and top with bacon.

Spaghetti Aglio e Olio

Ingredients

- 8 oz spaghetti
- 4 cloves garlic, sliced
- 1/2 tsp red pepper flakes
- 1/4 cup olive oil
- Salt to taste
- Fresh parsley, chopped for garnish

Instructions

1. **Cook Spaghetti:** Cook spaghetti according to package instructions; reserve 1/2 cup of pasta water.
2. **Sauté Garlic:** In a large skillet, heat olive oil over medium heat; add garlic and red pepper flakes, cooking until garlic is golden.
3. **Combine:** Add cooked spaghetti to the skillet, tossing to coat. If needed, add reserved pasta water to loosen.
4. **Serve:** Garnish with fresh parsley before serving.

Quinoa-Stuffed Acorn Squash

Ingredients

- 2 acorn squashes, halved and seeds removed
- 1 cup quinoa, rinsed
- 2 cups vegetable broth
- 1 cup black beans, drained and rinsed
- 1 cup corn, frozen or fresh
- 1 bell pepper, diced
- 1 tsp cumin
- 1 tsp chili powder
- Salt and pepper to taste
- Fresh cilantro, chopped for garnish

Instructions

1. **Preheat Oven:** Preheat oven to 400°F (200°C).
2. **Cook Quinoa:** In a pot, combine quinoa and vegetable broth; bring to a boil. Reduce heat, cover, and simmer for 15 minutes until liquid is absorbed.
3. **Mix Filling:** In a large bowl, combine cooked quinoa, black beans, corn, bell pepper, cumin, chili powder, salt, and pepper.
4. **Stuff Squash:** Place acorn squash halves cut-side up in a baking dish. Fill each half with the quinoa mixture.
5. **Bake:** Cover with foil and bake for 30-35 minutes until squash is tender. Garnish with fresh cilantro before serving.

Braised Beef Short Ribs

Ingredients

- 3 lbs beef short ribs
- 1 onion, chopped
- 2 carrots, diced
- 2 celery stalks, diced
- 4 cloves garlic, minced
- 2 cups beef broth
- 1 cup red wine
- 2 tbsp tomato paste
- 2 sprigs fresh thyme
- Salt and pepper to taste
- Olive oil for browning

Instructions

1. **Brown Ribs:** In a large Dutch oven, heat olive oil over medium-high heat. Season short ribs with salt and pepper, then brown on all sides. Remove and set aside.
2. **Sauté Vegetables:** In the same pot, add onion, carrots, celery, and garlic; cook until softened.
3. **Add Liquid:** Stir in tomato paste, then add red wine and beef broth, scraping up any browned bits from the bottom.
4. **Braise Ribs:** Return short ribs to the pot, add thyme, and bring to a simmer. Cover and transfer to a preheated oven at 325°F (160°C) for 2.5 to 3 hours until tender.
5. **Serve:** Remove thyme and serve short ribs with sauce over mashed potatoes or polenta.